Letters to

A Testimony of Healing from the Effects of Maternal Abandonment

Melanie Robinson

TABLE OF CONTENTS

DEDICATION

I want to dedicate this book to my angels: Ashley (my LP, Cashley), my love; Errol (Popa), my strength; and Delvin (Phatty), my sight. God blessed me with my babies when I needed them most. Mama loves you so much! To my daddy, for never trying to change me: I love you, and I miss you so much. Also, to my precious loves, my "SonnyWonny" (Mark3) and my "MarleyMar" (Marley), my grandkids. They are the most adorable little people I've ever met. Thank you all for your support and encouragement to finish this project. I wouldn't have done it without you!

ABOUT THE AUTHOR

Melanie Robinson is a mother, a grandmother, an author, a deacon, and a biblical teacher of life development for single mothers and young adults in California. She is the founder of Beauty for Ashes Coaching and a mentor to young women within her community. Melanie's mission is to guide men and women everywhere to take control of life's challenges.

Introduction

This book aims to enlighten women, men, and children who have experienced the effects of not having a physical, emotional, or mental connection with their birth mothers. *Letters to My Mother* is not meant to bring shame to my mother or anyone else's. This is also not about people who lost their mothers to death. These mothers were, or are, alive and have been separated from their children by physically leaving them, emotionally abandoning them, or having no mental connection with them. My personal passion is to help children learn to understand themselves and others who have lived or are living with the unspoken subject of the absent mother. Through this book, you will hear a child's heart and learn what it takes to empower yourself, to empower someone else, and how to turn your pain into power. I want you to come to a true understanding that the absent mother wasn't meant to break you but was really meant to build you.

The Absent Mother

A person with a mother who is fully and completely present could never understand what it feels like to not have a mother in their life. Few can even imagine how a mother could turn her back on the children she carried in her belly for nine months and then walk away without looking back. I know I can't, but maybe because it was done to me. The suffering I encountered was more than anyone could ever imagine and something I could never imagine doing to my own children. I am going to share with you what happens to a child who grows up without a mother.

This subject isn't often spoken about. So many websites, books, and countless other materials speak of fathers who leave their children, but there isn't much said about a mother leaving her children. I have always been willing to address things others choose to avoid. I've always been a quiet person, but it was in my heart to stay that way so that people would listen carefully when I did decide to speak. I always classified myself as a motherless child, though God has since told me to never say that again.

My mother left my sister and me to live her own life and seemed to have never looked back. I want to address the effects of this. I want to teach others how to get past this and live their best lives.

The pain of my mother's self-motivated move shook me to my core and paralyzed me, to the point of trying to end my own life at 9 years old. I remember thinking that if my mother didn't want me, why would anyone else? I felt unwanted and ashamed of the space I took up in the world. To this day, I'll never understand how I could commit this crime against myself, but my heart was filled with so much pain that I thought it was the only way to make it all go away. So I found some nail polish remover, and I drank it. I don't remember how much I drank, but I remember how nasty it tasted. After drinking it, I went to my room and got in bed so I could die. That was the first of three attempts, and I thank God every day that they failed. God later revealed to me that the devil knows he can't kill you, so he tries to get you to kill yourself.

I could not understand why and how my mother could leave me. I was seven, and my sister was eleven years old. I am not criticizing my mother or her decision to live her life as she felt she needed to. I am sharing this to bring awareness to the effects a child can experience due to the actions of an absent mother. I wish this hadn't happened to me, but because of it, I am the woman I am today—and I am pretty amazing, if I do say so myself!

I believe God's word is true when it states in Romans 8:28, "And we know all things work together for the good of those who love God, to those who are the called according to His purpose." I believe I was called according to God's purpose. I wouldn't change anything that happened, nor would I want to re-live it. I am confident that to become the woman, daughter, mother, and granny that I am now, I had to learn by going through difficult situations due to my mother's absence. I'm not perfect, but I love being a mother. I love it in a way that makes me believe I had to lose my mother in order for *me* to love my kids the way I do. In the way my mother couldn't love me. Given the place I am in now at 50 years old, I am so grateful she

5

left. Her absence blessed me with a gift that allows me to see the pain in people that others tend to miss.

I recognize the pain because I've seen it in the mirror for over 40 years of my life. I recognize that look of pain because I've seen it in my own eyes. The pain that I once had was visible through my body movements. The pain made me walk with my head down and shoulders slumped. I wouldn't make eye contact while speaking with others. When I talked, my voice sounded unsure—sometimes soft, other times inappropriately loud. I didn't like what I saw in the mirror. I was defeated.

I write this book as a survivor, and I want you to know that you can survive an absent mother too. I want you to know that God only allows you to suffer this type of pain because He already sees and knows you and your future, and He knows you will be okay.

Experiences

Before I get into the meat of the process of how I healed (of which more details will be revealed later), I would like you to take a moment to write about your experience. I will give you the steps I took to heal, so you can do the same and become victorious in this area of your life. Please take this time to share a few life experiences you had with or without your mother. Write your answer here:

_____

_____

_____

_____

_____

_____

_____

Feel free to share this book or the information you read with someone who needs it. Please understand that healing is a process, but you are worth the time and effort. You owe it to yourself and the child within you!

Voided Soul

Six years ago, on a Sunday morning, I was sitting in church feeling sad, emotionally hurt, and confused. I was 44 years old at the time. I sat in church Sunday after Sunday and attended Bible study on Wednesdays, and I was disappointed that I was afraid to interact with people. I knew they would reject me, so I never gave anyone the chance to get close. The rejection was coming from me... I didn't want what my mother didn't want, which was me. Sitting in a church feeling this way hurts horrifically. I was sad and confused, wondering why I was this way, and I couldn't shake it. As I had so many times in my life, I asked God, "Why did this have to be my life?" I had suffered most of my life with depression, self-hatred, no (not low) self-esteem, panic attacks, and fear. I knew something was wrong deep within me. I would watch other women smile, laugh, and make friends, and I would often wonder why I couldn't stay happy like them.

As I got older, I read self-help books and continued watching people, trying to learn how to be "normal." I just couldn't grasp the concept, which made me more sorrowful. I tried everything I could think of, such as drinking, partying, friendships, and intimate relationships. I tried to connect with older women to learn from them, and older women even tried to connect with me through motherly relationships. My countless failed efforts led me to more sadness. I didn't know what else to do, so I just stopped trying. I stopped searching. I stopped trying to understand. I completely shut down emotionally... and I even tried to drink my way out of my misery.

Then one day, my friend Shawn said to me, "Girl, you just need Jesus!" So I began looking for God on my own. I'd had a really unpleasant experience with the church before and hadn't been a member in 15 years. I told God I couldn't go back. I needed Him to show Himself to me in my own environment, and He did. I asked God, if He was truly real, to meet me where I was.

I prayed to God and read the Bible on my own. As I read, I found there was a lot of it I didn't understand. That led me to listen to and study preaching and teachings on television. But because I listened to so many different preachers, I started to get confused about what the foundation of a relationship with God was. That's when I felt God saying to me that it was time to return to the church. I knew I needed a pastor—my own pastor. Because I really didn't want to go back to church, it took a couple more years before I walked into my current church home, Cathedral of Praise International Ministries. I have to say, it was hard for me to transition into going to church regularly. Fortunately, I joined Ministries, volunteered, and a couple of years later I became a certified appointed deacon. That's when God truly began to move in my life.

In 2015, I felt the Holy Spirit moving mightily within me, and I cried out for God to heal my heart, and He did. I felt freer than ever! My negative emotions were gone. The shame, depression, self-hatred, lack of self-esteem, panic attacks, and fear were all gone! I was so happy. But then I heard the voice of God say to me, "You've got work to do." He told me I would still have to deal with the issues, to learn why they were in my life and how to overcome them. In my day-to-day living, I learned more about

Jesus and understood more about why He sacrificed His life on the cross, and His sacrifice was the confirmation that everything in my life would be fulfilled. I was healed emotionally; I just needed to learn how to live a healed life mentally.

That's how this book came to life.

Most of my issues were rooted in my mother leaving me. She never said goodbye. I was never told she wouldn't be in my life anymore. She never poured anything into the voided space in my soul that was meant just for her. Instead, a whole lot of negative emotions filled the empty space.

Me and My Mother

In 2000, my mother and I reconnected after 22 years apart. I was working at a truck stop as a security guard on the graveyard shift from 11 pm to 7 am. I was 29 at the time and had just had my oldest son. Even though I was in the middle of nowhere at this truck stop, I was never afraid. I wasn't going to church, but I had to have known that God was with me because I wasn't afraid to be around so many truck drivers at night.

During my shift one night, a truck driver approached me and said, "Do you know I killed my mother?"

At that moment, I was afraid, and I didn't have access to a phone. I was struggling as a single mother and couldn't afford a cell phone.

The truck driver told me he had killed his mother from the stress he had caused her. Then the man looked me in the eyes and said, "I don't care what your mother has done to you, but you need to forgive her."

When I tell you I got in contact with my mama as fast as I knew how... it was even faster than that. I hated my mother with a passion, but I needed to let go of my hate so God could freely operate and move in my life. The truck driver reminded me of the commandment that I *had to* honor my mother in order to be blessed. I understand now that forgiveness had to take place within me for God to do some things in my life. God knew she would leave this earth forever in less than five years after my encounter with that truck driver. God knew I couldn't live a proper life hating her after she died with no way to resolve the relationship. I will talk more about the importance of forgiveness later in the book.

Forgiving my mother really blessed me. I spent a single day with my mother before she died, and I am so grateful for that one day. We talked on the phone a lot and began a cool relationship. Then, just five short years later, I received a call from my father, and I knew before he even said it that my mama was dead. It hurt my soul so much. I only got to have five years with her, and though I am grateful for what I had, I wish it could have been more. We had so much in common; it was amazing. I miss what we could have possibly had. But I know my heart wasn't ready before I met that truck driver. God knew I needed that story to get my heart ready for her, and I pray this book prepares your heart with the peace you need to forgive your mother.

A Letter to My Mother

Dear Mom,

I'm writing this letter to share how losing you affected me as a person. Please know that I forgave you a long time ago for doing what you felt you needed to do. I'm not writing this to shame you or disrespect you. I will always honor you, because without you, I wouldn't be here.

God had a plan for me, and it was a good plan. I understand now that you had to leave for me to be the woman I am today. I wouldn't change a thing, but I wouldn't re-live it either. You had to be my mother in order for me to exist. There were things I needed, like your strength, passion, independence, creativity, way of thinking, and stubbornness (but I think I get that from Daddy too).

I love you, Mama. I hope you're proud of what I am trying to do. I want people to know what happens when a mother leaves and how it affects what they think of themselves and how they deal with life.

Sincerely,
Mel

In the Bible, Matthew 6:33 reminds us to "seek first the Kingdom of God and His righteousness, and all these things shall be added to you." In the middle of all my confusion and broken heartedness, this is the scripture I clung to. I really couldn't shake what I was living. I knew something was wrong with my heart, but I didn't know how to heal it. I thought I did okay in crowds (but I could have been wrong). I didn't trust many people, but I ended up trusting too much when I did. I didn't understand life at all. I thought I had done something terrible to either God or my mother, and that my life was my punishment. I couldn't understand why this had to be *my* life, but when I read this scripture (and yes, you can go to church and still have emotional wounds), it was all the instruction I needed. I didn't know everything that needed to be fixed with me, how to get started, or even if I should start at all, so I just read the word of God. I didn't always have a complete understanding of what I was reading, but I just kept going. If I looked for God, learned about Him and who He was and is, I knew He would add everything I needed in my life at the right time (His time). Applying Matthew 6:33 to my life is how I started my healing journey.

In order to heal, the very first thing to do is to forgive. You need to forgive your mother if she has done things she may or may not have regretted. Please know she did the best she could with what she had. Maybe she even wished she could change but couldn't heal her own wounds. Forgiveness doesn't mean what the person did was right. Forgiving a person is saying, "I release myself from what they did to me." It is deciding they will no longer have a stronghold over that part of your heart, mind, and soul.

Forgiveness is the freedom to control your heart and create something new. The Bible says we must renew our minds (Romans 12:2 NKJV). We must renew our minds from the old way of thinking to create a new heart. Some would think that holding on to the pain is paying that person—our mother—back. But you're only hurting yourself when you hold on to the pain. Marianne Williamson says it best: "Unforgiveness is like drinking poison yourself and waiting for the other person to die."

When I thought of my mother, I always just thought of her as my mom. *Nothing else!* But my mother and yours weren't just our mothers. Our mothers are women who had children. There is much more to them than the title of mother. My mother was a daughter, sister, aunt, and single mother (she left my father), but she was also Annie. She had dreams, desires, a childhood I know nothing about, pain, suffering, and her own life. She wasn't put on earth just to be my mom. We must understand that when our mothers leave us emotionally, mentally, and/or physically, it probably had nothing to do with us personally but everything to do with what was going on in their minds and lives. Just like me, my mother could have been suffering from traumatic events in her childhood that made her feel like walking away was the only way to have whatever she was searching for.

A Letter to My Mother

Dear Mommy,

Where are you? I've been here a long time, and I want you to come back. Come get me, mama. Did you say goodbye to my sister and me? I can't remember. Or did I forget on purpose because I didn't want it to be true? I don't want to believe that you would leave me forever. Or did you just not say goodbye because it wasn't supposed to be forever? What am I supposed to do without you, mama?

Sincerely,
Mel

A Mother

Mothers play a major, if not *the* major, role in their children's emotional, mental, and social development. They help children learn how to express themselves and teach them to understand and cope with their emotions. Children gain confidence through a mother's predictability, safety, and responsiveness. She is the first person her children learn to trust. A mother's role is more profound than even the mother herself knows. She is the foundation of her child's life and can affect everything her children think of themselves. Where the mother is in her life when she gives birth to her child can make or break the steps of the child's life.

A mother is pregnant with a child for nine months. During this time, the mother is emotionally connected to her child. Her voice is the one the child hears the most. The child can feel and sense the mother's acceptance or rejection while in the womb. The child is given to the mother for a reason. There is something in the mother that the child will need to be born into their purpose here on earth. No mother is given the ability to have a child by accident. These are my personal beliefs.

If your life with or without your mother was good or bad, please understand that this is to help you become the person you were meant to be. Another of my beliefs centers on the stages of development between 18 and 21 years of age. During that time, it becomes your responsibility to heal and build on what you have gone through until this point in your life. Your parents cannot repair any damage they have caused in your life. As you continue to grow, it is up to you to take what has been dealt to you and improve your life.

A Letter to My Mother

Dear Mama,

I've been here for a long time. Where are you? Are you going to come and get my sister and me? I don't understand why it's taking so long. Did you even say goodbye to us? I don't remember. Or did I forget on purpose because I didn't want it to be true? I don't want to believe that you would leave me forever.

Did you not say goodbye because it wasn't supposed to be forever? I feel alone without you, and I don't know what to do.

Sincerely,
Mel

A Child

Everybody is someone's child. You can deny your parents, but you cannot deny that you are someone's child. As a child, you are very vulnerable. You are open to everything that is presented to you. For example, a newborn baby is defenseless to the point that they need another person to help them in every stage of their development. You are born ready to soak up knowledge. Born to depend on the person who birthed you. You have no control over anything, including who your parents are, what they teach you, or how they treat you. The things you experience as a child will be joyous at times and very hurtful in other moments of your life. These experiences contribute to your future.

Often, as children, we look to our parents as superheroes or perfect people. But what many of us soon find out the hard way is that our parents were broken when they had us. Even though most parents want the best for us, few can follow through for us. Many children grow up with ill feelings towards their parents, often wishing things had been different. Parents have 18 years to shape us into productive people, but that is not how it happens for most of us.

My mother left. She sent us away, and I believed she owed me something. She owed me the mother figure other people had: her presence, protection, and nurturing. Once I understood that my mother couldn't be "motherly," my need for her added to the hate I already had in my heart.

Now it is up to you to grow into the person you want to be. Anything you see can be improved upon, and all the issues you may have incurred are due to your mother leaving you. It's up to you! Everything that seems to be a stumbling block can be turned into a steppingstone to something better.

What is your definition of a mother? Write your answer below:

_____

_____

_____

_____

_____

What is a child? Write your answer below:

_____

_____

_____

_____

_____

Please share your thoughts here about how your mother is or is not what you think a mother should be.

_____

_____

_____

_____

Different ways a mother can leave (abandon) a child:

1. Physically
2. Emotionally
3. Maternally

Abandonment is a strong word to use in the same sentence as Mother, but it needs to be said, and I am the right person to say it. Nobody talks about it, *ever*, and while it doesn't happen as often as fathers abandoning their children, it is still a real thing and needs to be addressed. This is needed so that the people who have experienced maternal abandonment can heal.

What does it mean to be abandoned? Tell me what you think abandonment means. Write your answer below:

_____

_____

_____

To be abandoned is to be left stranded by someone, and when that person leaves, they don't say goodbye or tell you why. They just leave you to wonder:

1. Why did they leave me?
2. What did I do wrong?
3. Why was I not enough for them to stay?
4. Do they love me? Or why don't they love me?

23

So many things can run through a child's mind when someone important to them physically walks away. These questions become much more powerful when the person who walks away is *their mother*. Mothers leave their children for many reasons, but the reason matters far less than the fact that they left.

For me, having my mother leave my sister and I shocked me to my core. From a very young age, I believed that if my mother could leave us, anyone could and would do the same. My mother's absence opened the door to things I couldn't understand for most of my life. There were things I didn't learn about until I was in my late forties. Yes, I said late forties—47, to be exact.

Trusting people has always been hard for me. I entered friendships wondering how it would end. I didn't believe that anyone would stay, so I often ended relationships so they wouldn't leave first. I didn't understand that I had control over the outcome of my life. It felt like my life made all the decisions for me, and it didn't like me. But I came to an understanding that I do have control, and while seeking and forming a relationship with God, He taught me that I could change by renewing my mind, finding a new way of thinking, and dealing with my life. I wrote this book so you won't have to suffer the things I did for as long as I did.

Okay, let's get into the second form of abandonment. Besides physically leaving, a mother can emotionally abandon her child/children. You can physically reside in the same home and have a relationship with her, but she can emotionally be gone. What does this look like? When a person removes themselves emotionally from you, there is a disconnection. When you're emotionally connected, unspoken needs will be searched for and met. For instance, as a parent who is emotionally connected, I know when each of my children is sad. They don't have to say a word because of my emotional connection with them. I know as a mother how to meet their emotional needs and connect with them to resolve whatever is in their hearts. All emotions are tended so they can mature. Unattended emotions transform into things that will separate you from your intended natural growth. In turn, a child may believe that their mother does not desire them. They may feel lost, as if they have been cut off from a critical source of nourishment, either suddenly or through a process of wearing-away (Mairanz, 2022).

The third form of abandonment I would like to address is maternal abandonment. What does this look like? It is "when a mother physically, emotionally, or psychologically removes herself from her children." She does this by ending or ignoring her responsibility to parent her children or ending her relationship with her children (Van Wyden, 2018).

A Letter to My Mother

Dear Mama,

What happened? What made you walk away from me and my sister forever?

Sincerely,

Mel

Defining Abandonment

There are more ways a person can be abandoned. The ones I'd like to address are emotional abandonment, mental abandonment, and physical abandonment. Emotional abandonment is when one may feel emotionally lost or disconnected from a loved one (Wikipedia contributors, 2022). Mental abandonment is the fear of becoming lonely; this can lead to people-pleasing tendencies and anxiety (WebMD Editorial Contributors, 2020). Physical abandonment is when there is a lack of supervision by a caregiver (Black M.S.W., Ph.D., 2010).

Do you know of any other ways a mother can abandon her children? Write them down here. Look up the definitions, along with how they may have affected you as a child and as an adult. Write your answer below:

_____

_____

_____

_____

_____

_____

_____

What are some effects of being abandoned by your mother? The child whose mother has abandoned him/her often develops low self-esteem. They experience confusion and may feel guilty, believing that something they did made her leave. Write your answer below.

Abandonment is at the root of many issues that children and adults have avoided confronting because they are unaware that this is the source of many of their problems. A great number of people that I have talked to simply say, "This is just the way I am!" or, "I don't need to deal with the past; it made me who I was meant to be."

I don't fully believe those statements. I use the word "fully" because I believe that when a person experiences any major issue, it is intended for them to overcome it and then help someone else to do the same. To brush the matter aside is like letting the painful issue win. I once met a woman who never dealt with this issue because she was afraid of the emotional part of moving through it. You shouldn't be afraid to face your emotions; they're yours, and to ignore them is like abandoning yourself, just like your mother did. You didn't deserve to be abandoned then, so please don't abandon yourself now. That's why I'm writing this book—so you will have evidence that becoming a better, happier version of yourself is possible!

For most of my life, I lived in sadness, wondering why *my mother* had to be the one to walk away from me. So many years ago, the answer I got back was, "Why not you?" Many years later, as I inched toward healing, I began to understand that God was not trying to kill me with pain. He was trying to build me up.

It's true enough that children of unloving and unattached mothers have common experiences. The lack of maternal care and validation warps the sense of self (Streep, 2015). Through my own experience and meeting others who have experienced similar maternal abandonment, I now understand that starting your life without a mother changes the person you could have been emotionally. I have also been in the presence of people who have had their mothers physically and emotionally present, and I know that having a mother doesn't mean everything will be perfect, but it does give you a better chance of being balanced mentally and emotionally. A mother's presence is fundamental! It is a necessary ingredient for a child to have an opportunity for a balanced life. A mother holds great control over her children's future, and if she chooses not to rise up to the gift of being a mother, the child suffers in one way or another, such as having trust issues, abandoning their future children, or poor self-perception.

A Letter to My Mother

Dear Mom,

I tried to die yesterday, but it didn't work. I woke up, and you were still gone. Why did you have to send me away? Why couldn't you let us stay?

Sincerely,
Mel

The Impactful Effect

To grow and thrive as an adult, children should feel loved and emotionally attached to their mothers. There may be some people that disagree with me, but I'm sharing my experience and that of several people I interviewed who also grew up without their mothers, either physically or emotionally. A mother's love, protection, and nurturing form the foundation of how you see yourself. I have seen this with my own children, comparing it to myself and what I have seen in other people without mothers.

Growing up without a mother affects everything. It affects what you think of yourself and what you think of others. She is your first relationship; she teaches you how to love, trust, and bond. She also teaches you what safety feels like and how to conduct yourself when receiving love. This relationship has an important role in what happens in your future friendships and courtships. It will affect how you let people treat you.

A Letter to My Mother

Dear Mommy,

How is it that I miss you so much, and I don't even remember us being in the same space as you? I don't remember anything about the six years we spent together. I don't remember your face, your voice, or your smile. I can't even remember if you touched me. Did you ever kiss me or tell me you loved me? What about holding my hand or combing my hair? There is nothing in my mind about you. Nothing! But I still miss you. I miss you so much that I can feel myself starting to hate you. Mama, I'll hate you for a long time, until I am 29 years old!

Sincerely,
Mel

My Father

In 2021, at the age of 50, I received more childhood information about myself and my sister. I didn't know it then, but my father had cancer. In 1973, even though my parents had divorced, my father was there from the beginning when my mother took him up on his offer to take us if the load was too much for her to bear alone.

After he took us in, he cared for our basic needs, but something was missing between my father and me. Right after his third wife died, he started preparing to die too. My relationship with my father was always distant, and we both knew it, but we became close during the last year of his life.

One day, I told my father about the book I was writing, and he said he had some information that I would need to add to the book. My father was a very quiet man and never shared his past with me unless I asked. Even then, he was very short and didn't give many details. So we set up a lunch date. We both enjoyed Macaroni Grill, so we had lunch there and I recorded the conversation because I wanted to be 100% present. He told me that he had told my mother that he would gladly take us if we were too much for her to handle. To his surprise, she took him up on his offer. He wasn't taking us away from her, just doing his part as a father. What my father didn't know was that my mother never told us we were staying forever. I don't remember him telling us either, but I remember I stopped taking calls from my mother at one point. In 1978, you did what you were told, but my father never made me talk to her. He let me feel whatever I was feeling, a hate that continued to grow as I became older.

My father told me stories about my mother that blew my mind. He talked about how she was only 16 when she had my sister and was still in school, but she graduated and they got married. My father joined the Air Force and would fly my mother to where he was stationed and back home to where she lived with her mother. My mother was the baby of her family, and she had four older brothers. She was very spoiled by everyone, my father included. He told me she was the love of his life, and when the marriage grew shaky, they agreed to have another baby to hopefully improve things.

My parents had a lot of friends. My mother's friends worked, but my mother was a stay-at-home mom and didn't want that life. Her desire was to attend college. My father gave her everything he thought would make her happy, but she wanted the freedom to explore the world and life independently. Having children at such a young age, she felt trapped.

Eventually, my father sent us to visit my maternal grandmother, but my mother decided for us to stay permanently and we never went back to my father. He was heartbroken.

I look just like my mother, and I have a lot of her ways. He said I walk and talk like her, and it was difficult for him to form a close relationship with me because he never got over her. When he looked at me, he saw and heard her. After that conversation, I was shocked but at peace because he answered all my questions. Everything made sense to my heart.

Most people probably won't be able to have this kind of conversation, and even if you do, it might not make your pain go away. I have grown to understand that my mother wasn't just my mother; she was a woman with dreams and desires. She wanted things for herself, and being a stay-at-home mother was not one of them. That's what my father desired: a traditional home like the one he grew up in. My mother joined the military and became a teacher. She traveled the country and I hope she found what she was looking for, but I don't think she did.

When I was 15, she tried to get my father back, but he had moved on with his life, and so had my sister and I. What she wanted was not what we wanted, and I let her know that when I saw her. I rejected her completely and didn't reconnect with her again until I was 29. She died five years after that.

A Letter to My Mother

Dear Mama,

You left my sister and me. We couldn't give you what you needed. You didn't say goodbye, so long, or see you later. Nothing. I was seven years old when you left me forever. You broke my heart, and I didn't want you to be in it ever again. I rejected people because you couldn't live your life with me. Why would you do that to your baby girl?

Sincerely,

Mel

A Topic Never Spoken

A mother leaving her child is a subject that most people don't know about or just don't talk about. When I began searching for information about mothers who abandoned their children, I couldn't find anything supporting this subject. I grew really frustrated, and that's when I knew I needed to put something together myself. It's amazing how God will allow what I have gone through to help people like me. Because of my mother's lack of skill, heart, compassion, or lack of strength to be a mother, I can help these people know they are not alone.

As I stated before, a mother can abandon her children and still be present in their lives. This would be emotional and mental abandonment. When a mother emotionally abandons her child or children, a wall is put up between her and the child. She can't tend to her child's emotional health or growth, which leaves the child to cope with the dangers of life alone. Children in this situation won't learn what to do with their emotions, causing them to suffer from anxiety, depression, and low (or no) self-esteem, just to name a few. The same is true with mental abandonment. There is often no concern from the mother about the child's mental health. The mother cannot connect with the child as a caregiver or the person required to train the child to deal with life's challenges. They leave their children to learn about bonding, learning the correct way to deal with problems or handle themselves, and every stage of life (Van Wyden, 2019). Mothers are our first relationships, and how a mother handles her child determines how the child's future relationships will unfold. Children learn how to trust from their mothers, and if they never trust their mothers, it's more likely that they will place their trust in people who mean them harm. Every relationship they form will be based on the abandonment.

The most important thing I learned on this journey was that my mother wasn't just a mother. I thought she was put on earth just to be my mother and had refused to do that, and I resented her for it. But I realized I was wrong. I understand that even more now since I've healed from her leaving my sister and me. My mother was her own person, and so is yours. They have to be, and they really don't have a choice if they want to be free. My mother needed more and wanted more than just to be a stay-at-home mom. She wanted to work and go to school. She wanted to travel the world, and she did. When she took my father's offer to take us, that was her opportunity to be free. She became a mother at 17 and, at 28, she had the chance to live the life she wanted... without us. What she didn't expect was for me to reject her the way she rejected me. My father never made me treat her like I wasn't hurt. Her sending us away and not saying goodbye separated my heart from hers for almost 30 years.

A Letter to My Mother

Dear Mama,

I can't forgive you. Because of you, I suffer every day. Missing you has turned to hatred. I've hated you for a long time because you sent me away and didn't come back for me. How do I let go of this? Right now, I don't care because you didn't.

Sincerely,

Mel

Forgiveness

Healing from the trauma of being abandoned by your mother must start with forgiveness. You must forgive her for not being able to care for and love you the way God intended. By forgiving her, you're not saying what she did is okay, nor are you saying you weren't affected by what she did or couldn't do. This forgiveness is for you and for you only. Holding on to the pain is hurting you more than you can imagine. By forgiving her, you can release the hold of what happened and make space to grow and heal. If you choose not to forgive because you don't think she deserves it or that it would let her off too easily, please know that's not how it works. Holding on to your hate is like drinking poison and thinking the other person will die. You must give yourself space to grow from the pain. Anything that has happened can be used as a steppingstone to something greater for you and your children. Renew your way of thinking and turn your pain into power. You are the only person who can start and finish this, but you don't have to do it alone.

- Relationships

Many people whose mothers have abandoned them suffer in relationships because their first relationship should have been with her. God set it up that way because women have nurturing hearts and a longing to care for people. It's something some women can't control. We've all been around women who played the role of being everybody's mama, and those whose mother was the opposite wished she could have been ours. Because our mothers could not give us the things we needed, we struggled in many relationships, even with our own children. When we were refused that bond that should have come naturally, we created a way to shield our hearts from the pain by making ourselves believe we didn't need it or didn't deserve it. Most of us existed in survival mode, and because this subject is not spoken about, we never learned how to get out. So many of us enter relationships thinking we must prove that we belong or run at the first sign that we didn't make the cut.

- Low Self-Esteem

Because most children long to please their mothers, mothers can groom their children into whatever they desire. A mother's approval or disapproval will shape her child's self-esteem. She gives her children the stamp of womanhood or manhood. Many adults today still need to be validated and look for it in all the wrong places because their mothers were supposed to give it. Low self-esteem can lead to so many other issues, too, such as poor hygiene, eating disorders, lack of confidence, the uncertainty of their own ability to make decisions, and anger issues.

- Insecurity

This is heavy. When a mother doesn't or can't function fully in securing her child's place in her heart, life insecurity is one of many issues the child may suffer from. Children who feel secure in their relationship with their mother have more balanced self-confidence and self-esteem. When insecure, children may be more prone to enter and stay in unhealthy relationships in a search for the security they should have found with their mothers.

- People Pleasers

If a mother can walk away, children may believe that anyone can walk away at any moment unless they make them happy. So most abandoned children will try to make everyone happy so they won't lose them. They give too much of themselves to people who don't deserve it. They stay in relationships that may be toxic, go out of their way to make sure their friendships are secure, and allow people to take advantage of them just so they don't have to suffer that abandonment again. Most children may think they have done something wrong and will try to do everything right for everyone they love.

- Walls

The walls that motherless children have built can be high and very thick. They are determined to never let anyone hurt them again and trusting people doesn't come easy. Remember that our mothers are the first people we learn to trust; if she walks away, we learn that nobody can be trusted.

- Attention Seekers

Abandoned children will do almost anything to get the attention they need. They need the validation that should have come from their mother. They are looking for what their mother wouldn't or couldn't give. They long for someone to look at them, to hear them, to tell them they're important enough to receive attention. These are just a few effects of not having the most important relationship in your life. Mothers are nurturers. They have a powerful role in their children's lives. A mother can shape a child's mind, heart, and soul.

As a mother and a grandmother, I know all children are different. I, too, received offers to give my three children away to family members when they saw my struggles, but because I suffered the effects of abandonment, that was never an option for me. My mother's abandonment made me strong, and I did everything I could to get us by. All my children are different, and it took different tactics to shape them into productive, loving, strong, caring, and independent people. I now thank my mother because I do my best to give my children what I desired as a child and even as an adult. I often wonder what a mother's love—my mother's love— would have felt like, and I wish I could have felt it. I have often asked God why He chose me not to have a mother's love, but the love I have for my kids and grandkids comes from the lack I experienced, and I thank God for that.

- Anger

This is something I've seen in a lot of abandoned children. Most of the time, it's not being able to let go of the hand in life you've been dealt. Most people believe they are owed something because they didn't have what everyone around them had: a mother. They feel like someone needs to pay them for the loss they did not deserve.

- Moving Forward

Let's talk about healing and moving forward in life. From this point on, you have a decision to make. You can either stay where you are emotionally and mentally, waiting for someone to fill all the voids in your heart, or take steps to become emotionally and mentally whole. I learned a while ago that if you're waiting for someone to come into your life and make everything better, you will wait for the rest of your life. If you're waiting for your mother to come and apologize and fix everything she broke, please know that can't happen and won't happen. She might apologize, but the only way that will happen is if she faces whatever issue she had, because if you ask any mother why, she will probably say, "I did what I had to do to survive." She may even say she did what was best for you. Whatever the case may be, no one can truly fix anything inside you. Only you are in control of that!

I have a motto: once you turn 18, it's up to you to fix anything that is wrong with you. You can't sit around and wait for someone to fix what they messed up. If they broke something in your life, it happened. Don't hand over your broken heart to someone who has already broken it! I know for a fact that you can improve any issue you're facing. Everything you've faced can and will work for your good. Don't expect anyone to do what you need to do for yourself.

A Letter to My Mother

Dear Mama,

I'm glad God chose you to be my mom. I understand I needed part of you in me to do what was planned just for me. My lessons and training started early for me. But I can truly say I have learned my lesson!

Daddy always told me I was just like you, and it used to make me mad. But now I smile because I can see you in me too after the stories Daddy told me. I'm proud of it! I am who I am because you gave birth to me and also because you walked away from me. I wouldn't change anything about our relationship... I just wish spending more time with you was part of the plan.

Sincerely,

Mel

Side Note: The book of John 10:10 NKJV, one of my favorite verses in the Bible, says, "The thief does not come except to steal, and to kill, and to destroy. I have come that they may have life and that they may have *it* more abundantly." I held on to this verse for dear life during my healing journey. I asked God to show me what He was about, and this is the scripture He put in my heart.

God doesn't have any evil in Him. He does allow evil in our lives, but He also taught me that everyone has free will. We can do whatever we want, and sometimes those things aren't good for us or for others. Sometimes, our actions cause hurt and suffering not only to ourselves but also to the people connected to us. My mother's decision hurt me, but I learned that God uses what hurts us for our good! Everything that has caused you pain emotionally and/or mentally can be exchanged for the better.

"To console those who mourn in Zion, To give them beauty for ashes, The oil of joy for mourning, The garment of praise for the spirit of heaviness; That they may be called trees of righteousness, The planting of the Lord, that He may be glorified" (Isaiah 61:3 NKJV).

I believe that whatever you've been through makes you into what God has planned for you to be. I refused to allow what happened to keep me in bondage. Like most people, my goal is to get to Heaven, but God gave me this life and wants me to enjoy my time here on Earth. Don't miss out on an abundant life because the hand life dealt you wasn't what you thought you deserved. You can create a good life for yourself. It takes hard work and determination, but you're worth it.

46

A Letter to My Mother

Dear Mama,

Today someone asked me, "What kind of woman do you think you would be if you had a mother?" Someone else asked, "Do you think your life would have been better had your mom been in your life?" I was surprised to be asked those questions, but some people feel good about trying to make others feel bad.

I never go beyond joking with my sister about how we would have turned out if you were around. I've always wished I could have had your love, but that's it. I believe I am exactly what God intended for me to be. After much hard work and healing, Mama, I really like me. It was hard for me not to have you in my life, but I made it without you.

I can't imagine a better life because the one I had didn't allow me to fantasize much. I wouldn't change anything, but I wouldn't re-live it either.

Sincerely,

Mel

Other Children Who Grew Up Motherless

I conducted interviews with others who grew up without their moms. When I say without their moms, I mean either physically separated or mentally neglected. She may have been physically there but didn't provide mental or emotional support to her child. I had people who were willing to share their experiences with me. I also used information I gathered from people who don't believe they are part of this group (I chose not to push the subject to these people because I don't have a degree, just my own life experience.) Everyone who was a part of this process was informed that everything they shared would be done anonymously. I will write about their thoughts and experiences to respect their privacy.

1. What do you think of your mother?

The general answer was, "She is selfish."
"She couldn't allow her child/children to get more attention than she got!"
"My mother was jealous."
"She wasn't capable of caring for us."
"She looked just like me. How could she not love me?"
"I didn't know that she was my mother until I was eight."

2. Tell me about your relationship with your mother (birth mother).

"I had no relationship with her."
"I can only recall a few moments of life with her."

"I lived with her till I was 11. Other than that, I have no memories to share about my mother."

"We had no bond."

"I was mad at my mother because she didn't protect me."

"She made me feel like I was a burden."

"I would physically fight my mother."

"I had no respect for her."

"She always put me down and never acknowledged any of my pain."

"She excluded me in every way possible."

"I felt completely alone as a child!"

"My mother dropped me off at my grandmother's when I was born. I didn't see her again till I was eight."

"She was a bully toward me and would say very hurtful things."

There are so many similarities between children who are now adults who didn't have their mothers. It amazes me. One of them is suicide. The crazy part about it is that when these children attempted to do it, there was no internet. This was back in the '70s and '80s. How would they have even known that suicide was an option? At least two of my interviewers tried this by the age of eight—yes, eight years old. A mother's presence and her absence are more powerful than most people realize. Mothers can mentally and emotionally kill their children.

- Drugs

People have all kinds of reasons for using drugs and alcohol. But for the children who didn't have their mother, they tend to do it in hopes of filling the hole in their hearts in the shape of their mother. But what many fail to realize is that neither drugs nor alcohol will make it better. They often don't realize that until much later or sometimes not at all. Doing these things seems to drown that pain for long enough to get through small spaces in their life, but it won't ever give them the assurance they are looking for. If anything, it makes things worse.

- Mothers Who Didn't Have a Mother

Becoming a mother after growing up without one is a major challenge. Most of us have no idea what to do with our children. A lot of the time, we are on the side of two extremes of motherhood. One is giving our children too much or, on the other hand, not being able to give them anything. Most mothers overdo it trying to prove they can do what they never saw or to give their children the things they didn't receive from their mother. The other side does exactly what our mothers did to us and abandon their children in one form or another. By facing your issues, healing your own pain, and turning your pain into power, you can go into motherhood fully prepared to end the cycle of abandonment on all fronts.

A Letter to My Mother

Dear Mom,

As I sit here today and write this letter, I can truly say that I'm writing from a healed heart and a place of forgiveness. For many years, I struggled with rejection and abandonment issues, and I was mad at you because we never had the mother-daughter relationship that I saw other girls have with their mothers. But these last two years, God has really been healing my heart, and now I understand that what the devil meant for evil, God turned around for my good. God used what the enemy did to make me a strong woman and a great mother. Rejection no longer has control of me. I want you to know that I forgive you and that everything I went through was not in vain. God is getting the glory from my story.

Sincerely,

Anonymous

Back to the interviews….

3. Do you think it affected you not having your mother?

On all fronts, everyone answered the same: ABSOLUTELY! It affected how they became women and what they accepted from people, including accepting things they shouldn't have just to be abandoned again. They suffered from low self-esteem. They felt they didn't have a voice, so they remained quiet when they should have spoken up. They didn't know about women's things such as hygiene, what to clean with, or how to clean themselves. It affected the way they thought about themselves.

4. How old were you when your mother left?

11 years old, 5 years old, from birth, another from birth, and 7 years old.

5. How old was your mother when she left?

26, 18, 16, 26, 23

6. Who raised you?

School raised a few of my interviewees.
"Life raised me."
"Nobody... Nobody raised me."
"My grandmother raised me."
"My father raised me."

7. How do you think it affected you?

"It broke me."

"I know I would have been a different person had she stayed or connected to me."

"My confidence is very low, and I view myself as less than others because of my relationship (or lack thereof) with my mother."

"I accepted her for who she was; she had her own issues."

"She did the best she could, but I never believed she loved me."

"She was very selfish."

"I talked to her a lot; I never missed her or called for her, never thought I was going home to her."

Let's look at another letter written by a child without their mother...

A Letter to My Mother

Dear Mama,

How are you? My sister and I are doing okay. As you know, we have been in California for about two years now, and you haven't called us once. Why? I know there is a time difference, but I'm waiting for the day that my stepmom says she talked to you and that you called to talk to us.

Anyway, I'm okay and school is going well. I'm enjoying my stepbrothers and stepsisters. Daddy doesn't see me that much because he works a lot. I'm writing to ask you if your mom, brothers, or friends ask about us. Do they ask where we are or if we're coming home? Do they ask why you sent us away? If so, what do you tell them?

My birthday is coming up! You haven't sent anything or called. Hopefully, this year you'll send me something or I'll get to hear from you. Maybe you'll send me something for Christmas. Well, tell Mu I said hello, I miss you, and I love you!

Sincerely,
Anonymous

Healing

I often say, "There are a lot of people who can live without God, but I cannot." I know all my help comes from God. The Holy Spirit changed my life by showing me who I was and what to do to move forward toward a balanced life.

I pray that you will talk to God and let Him know you want freedom from abandonment and trust Him to help you. It doesn't just apply to a mother leaving you, but to any area of your life that you want to heal from. Decide that you want something different for yourself. If you live with mental and emotional scars, they can be healed. If you learn about the things you face, you can change them.

Another thing I always say to myself and anybody dealing with an issue is that "if you want something different, you have to do something different" (Jack Canfield). And understand this: to heal from anything, it takes time. Don't get mad about the time it takes because the things you want to change have been a part of who you are for some time, if not for as long as you can remember. It will take time to reprogram your mind and your life. Even afterward, they will try to come back when you have trials. Let's use depression as an example: once you overcome it, there will still be situations where you will have to make yourself choose not to do what you used to do... You will literally have to make yourself walk in the healing process instead of doing what you would have done when depression was your only option.

Okay, let's get into the steps. Take your time with this; I promise you won't regret giving yourself freedom.

1. **Find a church.** Pray about where to go. Not every church is for everybody. Ask around, visit, and you'll know when you find your church home. Also, remember it's not about the people in the church (the congregation); it's about being fed by the preacher's word. You must remember that everyone is looking for something from God. They are not perfect and are trying to grow too. It's all about seeking the face of God so He can show you who He is and who you are to Him.

2. **Learn about yourself and what triggers you.** Watch what you do when you're upset. Do you eat? Cry? Get depressed? Does it turn people off? What happens when you get rejected? Do you cry, or wonder why you just can't fit in? Or, once accepted, do you give too much or put up walls? Take a personality test. Ask close people their thoughts about you (as long as they have your best interests in mind), such as your children or siblings.

3. **Start journaling.** Write what you are feeling and what you want to see. For the first part of your journaling, you may just talk to yourself about what you're feeling and what you'd like to do about it. Once you've done that, switch it up; only write what you want to see! (Side note: I was in a bible study one night and my pastor started talking about our future. He quoted Habakkuk 2:2 and focused on the B portion of the text that says, "Write the vision and make it plain.") Bishop Craig W.

Johnson explained how the brain works when you write: when you write something on paper, your brain tries to figure out how to make it happen. After I heard that, I began to think about what I was writing in my journal, most of which were bad things that had happened or if I was sad. Once I heard that message from the Bishop, I understood why the same issues were repeating themselves. From that day forward, I began to write about what I wanted to see. I stopped writing negative things and only wrote positive things. For example: I am happy, I love myself, and good things are happening for me. I am successful in all areas of my life. My children and I communicate well. I love the person I am. I trust my decisions concerning my life. I love myself the way I want love from others.

4. **Seek counseling and/or therapy, and/or a Life Coach.** I did all three! My pastor counseled me, and he is my life coach. I also went to therapy outside of church. You may not need all three, but I was so determined to live the life I read about in John 10:10. I have always talked God. I talk to Him openly because I figure He already knows what I'm thinking anyway, so I'll just say it... respectfully, of course (even though I know He hears the disrespectful version in my head). "I really want to go to heaven, but I want to enjoy the life You gave me on Earth too!" This is what worked for me.

5. **Forgive!** I know I said it earlier, but I must stress the importance of actively forgiving because YOU deserve it. It's not about letting someone off the hook. It's about letting yourself off that hook. Think about it. You've had to carry the pain, sadness, loneliness, and

heartbreak for a long time. Forgiveness opens the door to be free of those things. Don't allow them to keep you for any longer than they already have. You deserve this! Don't let what happened to you in the past control your future.

6. **Learn**. Learn about your issues and how and when they show up in your life. Doing research will give you an upper hand when dealing with your issues and moving into healing. Learning about these things will also help you once you've overcome them so that they won't overtake you again. One thing I wish I had known was that once you have overcome something, you must learn a new normal after you are healed (in your mind, heart, and spirit). You can't do the same things with your new confidence that you did when you had low confidence. When you are free from self-hatred, you will have to learn how to talk kindly to yourself even when you are down. This is true for any situation you're struggling with.

A Letter to My Mother

Dear Mama,

As I grew up, I wondered where you were every day and every night; I'd wonder if you were okay. All I ever wanted was for you to know that I loved you.

As time passed, I continued to miss you... thinking, "Will she ever come back?" I want you to know that you hurt me so badly by leaving me with my grandmother, but I forgave you. I forgave you over and over again and still wished you would come back. Night after night, crying, watching my friends with their mothers, hoping and praying for a mother-daughter day that I never got.

It saddens me that we never had a day just you and me, spending time, shopping, eating, or just showing each other love. But I had to get over it and realize that it would not happen. But I loved you so much, even in your absence.

As time moved on, you finally came around. I was so happy just to have you in my life, but you would still pull back, thinking I was feeling a certain way because you had been gone so long, but that was never the case for me. I loved you right where you were, and I told you that and showed you that love, but it never seemed like enough for you.

But today, I'm healed. I know you gave me everything you had; all that's missing is our mother-daughter day!

Sincerely,

Anonymous

Back to the interviews:

8. Have you said goodbye to the mother you always wanted?

This was pretty much the same for a few people: "Yes!" Because their mothers had left them physically or mentally when they were so young, many of them had given up on ever having what their hearts had always desired. Most just accepted that she couldn't give them what they needed.

But there are some who still long for the mother they always desired, and who are now mothers and fathers themselves.

"Saying goodbye to the mother I always wanted was something I couldn't do."

"I still desire what I wasn't allowed to have and still struggle with why I couldn't have my mother's love when I needed it the most..."

9. Does it affect how you interact with your children, and if so, how?

Everyone said, "Yes!" and that they tried to be the mother they always desired growing up. They overdo the things their mother lacked the ability to do for them. They give their children more material things than they need and spoil them in ways they think will make them happy. They also need a lot of reassurance that their children accept them for the mothers they are. They constantly worry that they really don't know what they are doing because they've never seen it done. For many, they have a fear that

60

their own children will reject them or that they will reject their children (repeating the cycle) or try to over-love them.

10. What do you find yourself doing to keep people in your life?

This was a deep question and brought up the fight or flight response in the interviewees, with a couple people answering almost the same: putting up with anything people give them just so they won't be abandoned again. Overdoing things for love and attention. A few have completely shut their hearts down and no longer care who stays or leaves. As one of them said, "If my mother left me, *anybody* could leave."

11. What did your mother think of you?

"She didn't think of us. She only thought of herself."
"She made the decision to walk away, and she stayed away, even to the point that she said, 'My children will have to make the first move if they want me in their lives.'"
"She thought I was a burden and reminded me of that often."

All of the anonymous "A Letter to My Mother" were written by adults. Most of them have healed and moved on, but a few were abandoned and didn't want to face it. Others still can't forgive their mothers for their selfishness.

Being abandoned is a life-altering situation and can affect you in many areas of your life, including the way you see and relate to yourself and to others. But you don't have to settle for what abandonment has caused you! You have the opportunity to exchange anything bad in your life for something better. Sadness for joy, anxiety for peace, hate for love, lack of confidence for strong confidence, and the list goes on. My prayer is that you will put in the work to achieve the blessing you deserve—freedom from what the past gave you.

- **My prayer for you:**

God, I thank You for having Your hand upon me to walk this path before those who are reading this book. I declare that You will bless each reader with wisdom, understanding, and peace. I pray for each heart and mind to be vulnerable unto You, to receive healing and deliverance from any pain they may be carrying. Assist them in casting each care upon You and the willingness to release their hurts and pains in exchange for Your unconditional love, comfort, and peace. In Jesus' name, Amen.

After everything I've lived and researched, the subject of maternal abandonment is still heavy on my heart. Maybe because I know I wasn't the first person to experience not having a mother, and I know I won't be the last. Everyone's experience is different, and people handle it differently. But what I know for a fact is that it changes you. It warps your mind and your emotions. I want people to understand that mothers have an amazing responsibility/opportunity with their children. Though the numbers are low, some women just can't carry the load; their children suffer, and possibly their grandchildren if the cycle is not stopped.

If you're a mother or a grandmother and this happened to you, you can still heal and make a change. It's never too late. If you are a mother who sees she has done this to her children, even if your children are grown, you can still make changes and bond with your children. Yeah, it takes work. No, it won't always be easy, but most kids always desire their mother's love.

In conclusion, I would like to thank everyone who took the time to read my heart on the subject of maternal abandonment. I would love to hear from you. I would love for you to share your story or leave a comment about how this book helped or enlightened you. Please reach out to me on social media at:

- Instagram: @beauty _for_ashes1971
- Facebook: Coach Melanie
- Twitter: @Melanie225
- By email at: beautyforashescoaching8@gmail.com.

You can also connect with me for help in your healing journey through my services as a Life Coach. Because of what I have gone through, I am able to assist you through your adventure.

Special Thanks

I want to thank my pastor, Bishop Craig W. Johnson, and First Lady, Demetria Johnson, of Cathedral of Praise International Ministries, for providing me the space to learn about God and who He is and a space to ground myself and heal. My mother (Annie) and daddy (Charlie), I'm so glad God chose you to be my parents! I want to thank Edna, my true friend who is always there for me, and the people I interviewed for their support and encouraging words. I also want to thank myself. Thank you for fighting and refusing to give up (even when I tried to)! #Icantstop #Iwontstop

Reference

Black, M.S.W., Ph.D., C. (2010). *Psychology Today*. Understanding the Pain of Abandonment.https://www.psychologytoday.com/us/blog/the-many-faces-addiction/201006/understanding-the-pain-abandonment

Mairanz, A. (2022). *Empower Your Mind Therapy, Relationships & Self Esteem: Flatiron, NYC*. Empower Your Mind Therapy. https://eymtherapy.com

Streep, P. (2015). *Psychology Today*. 8 Toxic Patterns in Mother-Daughter Relationships Despite the commonalities, there are differences. https://www.psychologytoday.com/us/blog/tech-support/201502/8-toxic-patterns-in-mother-daughter-relationships

Van Wyden, G. (2018). *Our Everyday Life*. Mother Abandonment & the Effects on the Child. https://oureverydaylife.com

Van Wyden, G. (2019). *Our Everyday Life*. Mother Abandonment & the Effects on the Child. https://oureverydaylife.com/mother-abandonment-the-effects-on-the-child-5196141.html

WebMD Editorial Contributors. (2020). *WebMD*. Abandonment Issues: Symptoms and Signs. https://www.webmd.com/mentalhealth/abandonment-issues-symptoms-signs

Wikipedia contributors. (2022). *Wikipedia*. Abandonment (emotional). https://en.wikipedia.org/wiki/Abandonment_(emotional)

CPSIA information can be obtained
at www.ICGtesting.com
Printed in the USA
LVHW071149261022
731595LV00010B/222